Make Your American Dream a Reality: How to Find a Job as an International Student in the United States

CEREN CUBUKCU

i

Legal Disclaimer:

This book and the information contained herein are presented solely for educational and entertainment purposes. The author and publisher are not offering it as legal or other professional services advice and the material is not meant to substitute legal or financial counsel.

While best efforts have been used in preparing this book, the author and publisher make no representations or warranties of any kind and assume no liabilities of any kind with respect to the accuracy or completeness of the contents and specifically disclaim any liability incurred from the use or application of the contents of this book. Neither the author nor the publisher shall be held liable or responsible to any person or entity with respect to any loss or incidental or consequential damages caused, or alleged to have been caused, directly or indirectly, by the information or programs contained herein.

All rights reserved. No parts of this book may be reproduced or transmitted in any form by any means, including electronic, mechanical, photocopy, recording, or otherwise, without the prior written permission of the publisher.

Throughout this book, trademarked names are referenced. Rather than using a trademark symbol with every occurrence of a trademarked name, we state that we are using the names in an editorial fashion only and to the benefit of the trademark owner, with no intention of infringement of the trademark. This book contains the author's own opinions and not those of anyone else, including those of the trademarked companies mentioned throughout the book.

Published by CS Publishing
7290 Investment Dr, North Charleston, SC, USA 29418

Printed in the United States of America
1st Edition: May 2013

ISBN: 605-86-1060-5
ISBN-13: 978-605-86106-0-6

DEDICATION

This book is dedicated to my family and my friends, in addition to everyone who has been part of my journey in the United States…

FREE BONUS ITEM

This book includes a free bonus audio interview. Please listen to this audio in addition to reading the book. You can listen to the interview by going to:

www.cerencubukcu.com/bonus

Or by scanning the below QR code with your phone:

ACKNOWLEDGMENTS

I want to thank my friends and my family for supporting me throughout my life no matter where I happened to be. I also want to thank my professors, advisors, counselors, coworkers, and others who helped me to grow personally and professionally and become the person I am today.

I especially want to thank a few people who helped me in the creation of this book. One of them is Oktay Sekercisoy, who was my advisor during my undergraduate years at Binghamton University. Sekercisoy, director for international partnership programs, is one of the few advisors I have had so far who always go above and beyond to help their students.

The other two people I want to thank are Lucy Amello, associate director of graduate career services at Bentley University, and Wendy D'Ambrose, director of graduate career services at Bentley University. Amello and D'Ambrose, who were my career counselors at Bentley, are two individuals who love what they do and who are very experienced in their fields.

Finally, I would like to thank Michael Miller, president of Culture Adapt and author of the book *4 Weeks to Your American Dream Job*, for providing his insights. Miller is a great entrepreneur whom I was fortunate to meet when I lived in Boston.

TABLE OF CONTENTS

ABOUT THE AUTHOR

Ceren Cubukcu is originally from Istanbul, Turkey, and moved to the United States in 2005 to pursue a degree as an international student. She received her bachelor's degree in information systems from the dual-diploma program of Binghamton University and Istanbul Technical University in May 2008. Under the rules of this program, she spent her freshman and junior years at Istanbul Technical University in Turkey and her sophomore and senior years at Binghamton University in Binghamton, New York, to complete the degree requirements of both schools. She graduated cum laude and received an academic award for excellence.

She found her first full-time H-1B sponsorship job as an IT advisory associate in KPMG LLP's New York City office six months before her graduation. She worked in this position for a year, serving financial institutions on Wall Street.

In August 2009, she received a scholarship from Bentley University in Waltham, Massachusetts, to study for her MBA. She worked as a cyber law research assistant while pursuing her MBA. She received her MBA with distinction in May 2011.

She received three H-1B sponsorship job offers before her graduation. After her MBA, she worked as a business systems analyst at Merkle Inc., a customer relationship management agency in Greater Boston Area for two years. She recently founded her consulting business to help more international students find jobs in the US in addition to her digital event ticketing platform. She is also a published author.

PREFACE

This book is for international students who are actively looking for jobs or internships in the United States. I decided to write it because my peers were always asking me the question: "How did you find a job as an international student in the United States?" There is no direct or one right answer to this question. Finding a job is a process, and this process will be different for everyone.

When I first came to the United States, I had no idea how to find a job here, so I had to educate myself on everything, such as the work-authorization rights for international students, how to write a great resume, how to interview, etc. I used many resources while learning all this. I went to conferences, researched the Internet, asked people, and read different books. This book is a compilation of the information I have gathered so far related to how to find a job in the United States as an international student. Therefore, readers can find this information in one place and don't need to search several different places as I did.

I went through this process when I was graduating from both my undergraduate and graduate programs. I actually got my first job offer six months before I graduated from my undergraduate studies. After working for the sponsoring company for a year, I went to graduate school and I again had to go through the same process. Before I graduated, I got three job offers, and all of them were from sponsoring companies. That's why I wanted to share my experiences with other international students so that they can also find sponsoring jobs in the United States.

I have been in this position twice, so I understand your situation. I know what your problems are because I faced the same problems too. There are many steps that you can take to overcome these problems and to ensure that you are on the right track. It's not as hard as you think. In this book, I will show you those steps, and I will also share with you the mistakes that I committed so you won't repeat them. After reading this book, you will have a clear path for your job-search process as well as be able to define a strategy for yourself. I did it and there is no reason you cannot do it as well...

1 KNOW YOUR WORK-AUTHORIZATION RIGHTS IN THE UNITED STATES

If you want to work in the United States as an international student, first it is very important to know your rights. Thus, my opening chapter is designed to give you an overall idea of the types of work authorization available to you. However, I am neither an attorney nor a school official trained on the subject matter. The information below is drawn solely from my personal knowledge that I learned by researching and listening to experts at employment conferences in my schools. By the time you read this book, some of this information may have changed, so I would recommend consulting your school's international student office for the most up-to-date information.

Although most students state that they know their work-authorization rights in the United States, school officials and career counselors do not agree with this assumption. Oktay Sekercisoy, director for international partnership development at Binghamton University, says that "students that I talk with are not aware of their authorization rights because they don't know the system." Michael Miller, president of Culture Adapt, also thinks that international students do not know their work-authorization rights. "I think that's the biggest gap," Miller says. "I've done a couple of visa or immigration issue events and they're always really, really packed and you would think that most universities cover that, but it's not covered well at all and it's not simplified."

Experts emphasize that it is important for you to know what your rights are and that international students can get work authorization in the United States if they fulfill certain requirements. There are several different work authorizations available to international students. The most common ones are CPT (Curricular Practical Training), OPT (Optional Practical Training), and H-1B. I will discuss these in detail in the rest of this chapter.

On-campus and off-campus employment:
First, let's start with where you can work. You can work either on campus or off campus. It is easiest to get work authorization for on-campus employment. Once you have a letter of employment, you should go to your school's international student office and fill out Form I-9 (Employment Eligibility Verification) and possibly a few other forms as well for tax purposes. Also, if you are going to work on campus, you can work anywhere you want. The job doesn't need to be related to your specific area of study. You can work in the library or in the computer lab, or you can work as a teaching assistant. You name it, anything is possible.

For working off campus, there are more rules and restrictions, as well as different types of work authorizations. For example, if you want to work off campus to gain work experience during the semester, when classes are in session, some schools require you to register for a credit course in order to get your internship authorization. This authorization is called CPT (Curricular Practical Training) and the credit is called a CPT credit. Also, in order to be authorized for CPT, you have to be in the United States for at least two consecutive semesters and you have to be a full-time student. I will discuss CPT in more detail in the upcoming pages. Moreover, if you have financial difficulties arising from unforeseen circumstances beyond your control and you have been an F-1 student for at least one academic year, you can get authorization to work off campus during the school year up to twenty hours per week. As you can see, although there are some restrictions, you can still work both on campus and off campus when school is in session.

When school is not in session, for example during winter and summer breaks, you can certainly do an internship if you have been in the United States for at least two consecutive academic semesters. Your school's international student office should know the rules and regulations of work authorization for international students, so please consult with them or go to their website for more information. If your school doesn't have a comprehensive website, I would recommend you check out the website of my undergraduate school, Binghamton University. Follow the links to the page of the International Student and Scholar Services (ISSS). The ISSS website has lots of information about employment for international students.

Difference between J-1 and F-1 visas:
While you can get work authorization for on-campus or off-campus jobs, you should remember that there are different regulations for J-1 and F-1 students. J-1 students have more work restrictions compared with F-1 students because of the type of visa that they hold. A J-1 visa is known as a visitor exchange visa, which is available to students who are supported substantially by funding other than personal or family funds, such as funding from their own government or from an international organization. Some J-1 students are subject to the two-year home country physical presence

requirement, meaning they have to return to their home countries for at least two years after they complete their studies. This requirement applies to you if your studies are on the "skills list" put out by the Department of State. You can check the Department of State's website for more information on this or consult your school's international student office.

The F-1 visa is available to full-time students who have been accepted to a US school. I was an F-1 student, so I am not really familiar with J-1 work-authorization regulations. Some of the information I discuss in this chapter may only apply to F-1 students. I would recommend to J-1 students to consult with the international student office in their school or with an immigration attorney to get more details on the rules and regulations. Next, I will discuss the work authorization rights in detail.

What is CPT?
CPT stands for Curricular Practical Training and it is an off-campus work authorization usually for internships. CPT is valid only for the period that it has been authorized for. For example, if you are going to work during the fall semester, then the school can authorize it for the entire fall semester while you are also studying. An important thing to note is that you can only work up to twenty hours when school is in session, meaning during the fall and spring semesters.

You can apply directly for CPT through your school. You need to have a job offer from an off-campus employer and this job must be directly related to your field of study. It takes around two weeks for the school to issue you the CPT authorization, which is a new CPT I-20 stating your employer on the third page.

What is OPT?
OPT stands for Optional Practical Training. It is a type of work authorization for employment related to your field of

11

study. OPT is a benefit for holders of valid F-1 visas and it is valid for twelve months. To be eligible, you must have completed one full academic year of study in the United States. Most F-1 students use this type of work authorization after they graduate. With your OPT authorization, you can work for any employer, but you can only work in jobs related to your major. You cannot work in jobs that don't relate to your major or to the degree that you have studied. You can also work part-time or without getting paid. When you are authorized for OPT, you receive an EAD (Employment Authorization Document) card so you can start working for employers.

You can apply directly for OPT through your school. You need to fill out the Form I-765 (Application for Employment Authorization) and bring a recommendation from your academic advisor. You also need to pay a fee and provide personal information, such as a copy of your passport's identity page, previous I-20s, and your picture. Please consult your school's international student office for the most accurate application process and guidance. An OPT application takes around three months to process, so it is recommended that you apply as early as possible. You can apply as early as ninety days before your graduation and as late as sixty days after your graduation. I recommend applying at least two months in advance before completing your degree. For example, if you are completing your degree in mid May, then it is best to apply around the first two weeks of March to avoid any unexpected situations. I applied for OPT at the beginning of March during my senior year as an undergraduate and, surprisingly, I got my EAD card within a month. However, I noticed that my gender was not listed correctly in my EAD card, so I had to send it back. Fortunately, I received my corrected EAD card in mid May, just in time for graduation. Thus, in order to have some room for unexpected events, I recommend applying for your OPT authorization as early as you can.

Lucy Amello, the associate director of graduate career services at Bentley University, reminds students that if they graduate and don't apply for OPT within the OPT application time frame and find later on that they want to apply for it, there is no way back. Therefore, make up your mind early and apply as early as you can.

The most frequent question asked by international students when applying for OPT is, "Do I need to have a job offer to apply for OPT?" The answer is "No." You don't need to have a job offer to apply for OPT. You can apply without a job offer and you can continue to search for jobs after you send in your application. One important thing to note is that you cannot start working without your EAD card. Also, even if you have your EAD card, you cannot start working until the day written in your EAD card, which is generally the date you stated in your OPT application. However, keep in mind that there is a limit to the number of days you can be unemployed while on OPT and that limit is ninety days. Thus, make sure that you start working within ninety days of the start date listed in your EAD card.

Also, it is not recommended to travel outside the United States while your OPT authorization is pending, because then you may not be allowed to reenter the country. You can only travel outside the United States after you get your EAD card and a job offer to return to from your prospective employer. It is best to consult your school's international student office before traveling outside the United States on OPT.

<u>What is the seventeen-month OPT extension? Can everyone get this extension?</u>
The seventeen-month OPT extension is an additional work authorization to your twelve-month OPT. However, this extension is not available to everyone. It is only available to science, technology, engineering and mathematics (STEM)

graduates. Also, in order to get this extension, applicants must be already working in OPT status in paid employment. Volunteer positions are not allowed and the applicant must be employed by an employer registered with the "E-Verify" federal employment-verification system.

You can apply for an OPT extension the same way you applied for OPT. You apply for it through your school's international student office, and the office issues you a new I-20 for the OPT extension. Afterward, you fill out Form I-765 and submit it with a fee. You have to apply for your OPT extension before your current twelve-month OPT expires. It is best to apply three to four months in advance of your current OPT expiration date to avoid any problems.

What is H-1B?
H-1B is a nonimmigrant visa that allows foreigners to work for a temporary amount of time in the United States. For example, if you are already working with an OPT authorization and your employer wants you to continue working there after your OPT expiration date, then the company should apply for an H-1B visa for you so you can keep working there.

Oktay Sekercisoy of Binghamton University states that students should use OPT to talk with prospective companies to explain the situation that they can work with their OPT authorization for one year and then, after one year, they can use OPT as a bridge for their H-1B application. But he complains that many students that he talked with are not aware of how this system works.

Unlike CPT and OPT, you cannot apply for H-1B yourself. Your employer should apply for you. The reason for this is that the H-1B visa is tied to your sponsoring employer as well as your job roles and responsibilities. Therefore, it is best to start working with an OPT for an employer and then convince the employer to sponsor an H-1B visa for you. Also, H-1B jobs usually require a bachelor's degree or higher, so you should have completed at least a bachelor's degree. You can get more comprehensive information about H-1B visas from the US Citizenship and Immigration Services website (www.uscis.gov).

Now let's take a look at the most frequently asked questions about H-1B visas by employers and students.

1) Does H-1B have a cost to the employer?
This is the first question potential employers typically ask if they are not familiar with the H-1B process. I recommend that you should be up-front about it and let them know that H-1B has a cost to the employer, but this cost is very minimal compared with the value that you will bring to the employer. The costs associated with H-1B visas are fees that need to be paid to the government and to the attorneys for filing the application. Since an H-1B application is more complex compared with OPT, generally attorneys fill out the application and submit it.

2) When is best time to apply for H-1B?
The H-1B fiscal year starts on October 1, and the application period for that fiscal year starts on April 1. For example, if you want your H-1B visa to start on October 1, then it is recommended for your employer to file your application by April 1. The reason for this is that there is a quota on the number of H-1B visas that can be issued per year. If you apply later, for example, in August, then you may not be able to get the H-1B visa for October 1, because all of the visas may already have been issued.

3) How many H-1B visas are available per year?
There are only 65,000 visas available to foreign nationals per year. In addition to this, there are 20,000 visas available to foreign nationals holding a master's degree or higher. If you

only hold a bachelor's degree, then you are subject to the 65,000 visa quota. If you hold a master's degree or higher, your application is filed under the 20,000 visas available for foreign nationals holding higher degrees. If all of the visas under this category are filled up, then you can also get an H-1B visa under the other category that has 65,000 visas available. This means that if you hold an advanced degree, you have more chances of being issued an H-1B visa. However, if you work for a university or a nonprofit research institution, then you are not subject to any visa limitation. Your employer can apply for an H-1B visa for you anytime.

4) How long is the H-1B visa valid?
An H-1B visa is valid for three years, but it can be extended an additional three years, meaning that you can work for six years under an H-1B visa.

5) Can I travel while my H-1B visa petition is pending?
It is not recommended to travel outside the United States while your H-1B visa petition is pending, because you are changing your status from OPT to H-1B, so you may not be able to reenter to the country before your H-1B visa petition is authorized and before you get an H-1B visa stamped to your passport. If you need to travel outside the United States while your H-1B petition is pending, it is best to consult with an immigration attorney to avoid any issues.

6) What if my OPT authorization ends before October 1, which is the start date of my H-1B visa?
One important thing to note is that if you are working under an OPT authorization and it ends before October 1 but your employer files for an H-1B visa for you that starts on October 1, before your OPT authorization expires, then your OPT authorization is automatically extended. For example, if your OPT authorization expires on July 1 but on April 1 your employer applies for an H-1B visa for you and that H-1B starts on October 1, then your OPT authorization is

automatically extended from July 1 to October 1 so you can keep working for your current employer. It is recommended to let your school's international student office know that your employer applied for an H-1B visa for you and that your OPT is extended so that a school official can issue you a new extended I-20. However, if your H-1B visa petition is rejected, then it is best to consult with the attorney who submitted your application to see what went wrong.

7) Can I change jobs while I am on an H-1B visa? Can I relocate to a different office while on an H-1B visa?

Yes, you can change jobs or relocate to a different office while on an H-1B visa, but if you are changing employers, you should get your new employer to petition for a new H-1B visa for you. The same goes with different job roles and different office locations. If you are changing to a completely new role or to a new office location under the same employer, then your current employer needs to submit a new H-1B visa petition for you. However, since you are already working under an H-1B visa, you are not subject to any date limitations or quotas this time. I still recommend, though, that you to work with an immigration attorney in this situation.

8) Can I work part-time with an H-1B visa?

Yes, you can work part-time or full-time on an H-1B visa. However, you need to get paid while working under H-1B, and it cannot be voluntary work.

2 HIRING PROCESS IN THE UNITED STATES

Now that you know your work-authorization rights in the United States and can educate your potential employers that you can in fact work in this country, let's look at how US companies hire workers. In this chapter, you will learn the US hiring and recruiting culture so you can start preparing to build your job-search strategy.

What is the hiring and recruiting process in the United States?

In the United States, the hiring and recruiting process involves the steps of attracting, screening, and interviewing candidates for an open position, and then "onboarding" a new employee for an open position. This process can take as short as a week or two and as long as a few months. This depends on the company's urgency to fill the position. If the company needs to fill an opening immediately, then it takes less time. However, in general, this process takes around one month to two months.

The screening process is a way for HR employees to determine and find the right candidates to interview. It's the first process after you apply for a job. Basically, employers go through the resumes submitted for an open position, screen them, and find the right candidates to call for interviews.

The interviewing process changes from company to company, but usually the first stage is always the phone interview. I noticed that most of the international students try to avoid doing phone interviews because they think that they would not be able to express themselves well enough to impress the employer. You should never reject an interview.

Oktay Sekercisoy of Binghamton University also recommends that students take any interview that they have been called for because it is an opportunity for them to show their personality. "They are avoiding those kinds of phone calls or Skype interviews," Sekercisoy says. "Don't do that. You have to show that you are a person that's not afraid to speak and you are taking initiatives."

Employers ask you to do a phone interview with them so that they can screen you. If you pass that phone interview, you are invited to the company's office for another interview, and you may go through a couple of different interviews with different people for a period of time during the company's interview process. That is generally called an on-site interview.

On-site interviews can take as short as half an hour and as long as a full day and may involve many different people. They can also include case interviews, presentations, behavioral interviews, or technical interviews. The interview process depends on the company and what it wants to do. It is best to ask what to expect during the interview process before going there so you can be prepared for any situation. I will talk more about the interview process in Chapter 6. For now, let's examine how and when corporations hire in the United States.

How do corporations hire in the United States and when do they hire?

Corporations hire in many different ways. The most traditional way of hiring is posting an ad for an open position to multiple different places, such as career websites or newspapers and screening the candidates who apply for this position. When a candidate's skills match a company's desired job profile, the candidate is invited for an interview and a job offer may be extended to him or her, or the company may reject the candidate and interview others.

However, this doesn't mean that companies always hire this way. In some cases, corporations hire through referrals. For example, one of the firm's current employees may refer you for a particular job if that employee thinks you are a good fit for that position. This actually increases your chances of getting hired since someone in the company already approves you. Another way corporations hire is through employment agencies. Corporations hire these staffing agencies to find them suitable candidates for their job openings. Nowadays, companies also use social media websites such as LinkedIn to recruit new employees. I will talk about the importance of using LinkedIn efficiently in the upcoming chapters.

It is important to note that companies do not hire the same way. Also, the same company may hire differently for different positions.

Companies usually hire whenever they have an opening for a certain job. However, I noticed from my own experience and from other people's experiences that the busiest months for recruiting are usually March, April, and May. The reason for this is that most companies get their annual budget for recruiting at the end of January or in early February, and they do preparations during February and start hiring in spring. Also, most students graduate during May, and that is also another factor affecting recruiting. Some large enterprises, such as the Big Four accounting firms, consulting firms, and financial institutions, hire students during their fall semester, so fall is also a very busy season for student hiring.

You should learn when your target companies are recruiting. Lucy Amello of Bentley University states that some companies, such as the Big Four accounting firms, start their hiring process very early on in the fall. The leadership rotation programs hire very quickly in the fall as well because they have a very extensive interview process. For example, when I was about to graduate from my undergraduate studies, I mainly applied for jobs at very large enterprises only, and they were doing on-campus recruiting in fall. Therefore, the best option for me was to network with the employees of these corporations during the school job fair and information sessions in order to get an interview, and that is what I did. I landed a good amount of on-campus interviews with these corporations and I passed a majority of them and got invited to their headquarters for the second round of interviews. Finally, I landed a job at KMPG's New York City office as an IT advisory associate six months before my graduation.

However, when I was graduating from my MBA studies, this time I wanted a change and targeted small and midsize corporations in order to get more job responsibilities. As a result, during my first semester, I didn't have as many interviews as I had when I was graduating with my undergraduate degree. However, I was very busy interviewing during my second semester. The reason for this is that many of the small and midsize corporations recruit students during their second semesters, as opposed to large enterprises that recruit students during their first semesters.

I didn't have this information previously because no one had told me. If I had lost my hope and given up during my first semester because I hadn't had as many interviews as I had when I was an undergraduate, I would never have been able to get three job offers to choose from. The key here is to know when your targeted companies are recruiting and make a plan accordingly. Also, do not to give up on your job search too quickly unless you believe you did everything you could possibly do correctly.

Oktay Sekercisoy of Binghamton University also believes that international students give up too quickly on their job search. He says that "they are discouraged very quickly that they cannot do this. They cannot go through this process because they have the understanding that the minute they graduate, they will get a job, which is not true for anybody anymore. Maybe it was true in the past, maybe it is true in their country, but not in the US context. I'm sure there will be some people in your classes, in international students' classes, who find jobs before they graduate. It still happens, but it's not as prevalent as it was in the past. Don't get discouraged if you don't find a job right away."

You shouldn't get discouraged too quickly and give up on your job search unless you believe that you did everything right that you could possibly do.

Types of hiring:
There are two types of hiring: internal hiring and external hiring.

Internal hiring is hiring someone who is already employed in the company. For example, if you are already working for a company under job A but you switch to job B under the same company, then you are an internal hire. You are hired for job B internally.

External hiring is hiring someone from outside the company for an open position. Almost all of you will be external hires when you are extended job offers, if you are not already, or if you were not previously employed with that company as an intern.

<u>Do companies and HR professionals hire only locally?</u>
No, HR professionals do not hire only locally. They tend to hire locally, though, but if they identify a potential candidate who is a good fit for a job at another location, they can refer them to that location's HR personnel as well.

Companies also don't hire only locally. They generally hire globally. For example, there are lots of companies that have offices in other countries. If they identify a potential candidate here in the United States, they may say, "We want to hire you for our office in country X." It is up to you if you want to go to country X, but it may be an option for you to consider if you like the position and the company.

Some companies also have some global programs that require you to work a few months in one location and a few months in another location, and they hire for those types of programs from anywhere in the world. Since we are living in a global economy, recruiting is also generally global.

Companies hire from anywhere, but if you are majoring in finance and looking to work in a bank, then you have better chances of finding your dream job if you study around the Greater New York area. Why? Because the capital of finance in the United States is New York City. Similarly, if you want to work in a high-tech company, you have better chances of finding your dream job if you are studying in California. If you want to work as an academician, go to medical school, or work in a medical company, then you should be in Boston. In the United States, pretty much each region has its primary sector, so it is always better to be in a location where you have more chances of attaining your dream. For example, I have a very close friend in Boston and her expertise is in the construction field. Although she is a green card holder, she cannot find the job that she is looking for because there are only approximately ten construction companies in Boston, whereas if she lived in California or in Texas, where there are at least fifty different construction companies, she would have more chances of finding the job that she is dreaming of. Don't limit your job opportunities; apply for jobs in other locations as well. If you have enough resources, go to different locations and attend the career fairs in those locations.

Oktay Sekercisoy of Binghamton University also agrees that international students should not limit their job search to a certain geographical area. "They either want to be in Manhattan or they want to be in a big metropolitan area, and they don't want to go to small cities. They don't want to go to small organizations. That's a big mistake. For your new job, you should be ready to work in a rural area, if that company is giving you a job. You should not just look at the big cities. You should not just look at New York."

Campus recruitment:
Campus recruitment is an effort made by employers to recruit students from their college campuses before they even graduate. Campus recruitment is one of the best ways to meet with potential employers and to let them know that you are a good candidate for the position you are interested in. Don't forget that you always increase your chances of getting hired whenever you meet with employers face-to-face rather than just applying online to job postings. In the upcoming chapters, I will talk in more detail about how you can meet with potential employers and what you need to say when you actually meet with them.

Campus recruitment usually involves information sessions held by employers to explain what they do and what positions they are looking to hire for; it also involves job fairs and interviews. I am originally from Turkey, and universities in that country usually have career days and employers come to the campuses to hold information sessions, but then you have to apply for jobs with these companies through their online application systems. For this reason, when I first came to the United States, I didn't know anything about job fairs or what to do at a job fair. I am sure there are many international students who feel the same way. Thus, I want to explain everything I have learned so far throughout this book.

A job fair is a career fair. It's a fair for employers to meet and identify potential job seekers. In this case, you are the potential job seekers. At a job fair, there are many different types of employers looking to hire for many different positions. Therefore, I always recommend that job seekers study what companies are coming to the job fair and what positions they are hiring for so you don't waste your time in the fair trying to identify which companies to talk with. If you come to the job fair prepared, you can directly go to the booths of the employers that you are interested in and meet with them face-to-face and describe your interest in the companies and the positions they are hiring for.

After the job fair, some companies want you to apply to their job postings through their career websites or through your school's recruiting website for students. Thus, you should take notes during the job fair so you know which companies to follow up on and how.

Companies post jobs almost anywhere nowadays. They post jobs on their career websites, on college career websites, on LinkedIn, and on other career websites such as Career.com or Monster.com. You can also look at these postings before the career fair. If you apply for one of these positions and the position is not one of the advertised positions in the career fair, you can always ask the recruiters if they can consider you for the position that you already applied for. You should always come prepared to a job fair to get the most out of it.

<u>Hiring by referral and how LinkedIn can help you:</u>
If someone you know is already working in a company which you are targeting and that person sees a job posting he or she thinks you're a good fit for, then that employee can refer you for that job posting. If you get hired, the employee may get a financial reward or a bonus from the company for helping the recruiting efforts.

Hiring by referral can work for you if you expand your network. The network can help you in a greater way by giving you access to more people who are actually working for specific companies and who can refer you to the job openings in their companies. This greatly increases your chances of getting hired, and it is also good for the employee referring you because he or she may get a financial reward if you get hired.

LinkedIn is a great way to get introduced to new people. You can build your network in LinkedIn and connect with other people. If there are companies that you are interested in and you see that you have second-degree and third-degree contacts in those companies, you can ask to be introduced to those people and then eventually you can ask them to refer you to their HR department for the job that you are interested in. For example, after one of the students I am mentoring looked at my contacts and found out that I have a connection in a company that he is interested in, he asked me to introduce him to that person so he could be referred to the HR department in that company. You can also connect with potential recruiters on LinkedIn and you can even sometimes e-mail or send a message to them directly.

Also, your experience is listed on LinkedIn, so it's a great tool to show your resume and maybe you can even give the link to your profile when you apply for jobs so potential employers can also check out your LinkedIn profile to have a better understanding of your credentials.

In LinkedIn, you can also list your references. For example, if you have previous internship experience or even previous full-time experience, you can ask your previous supervisors to write references for you in LinkedIn so anyone can see them.

I recommend that everyone use LinkedIn, whether you are looking for a job or not. It's a great way to stay connected with people on a professional level and to increase your chances of having more visibility.

Recruitment agencies and headhunters:
Recruitment agencies and headhunters are third-party HR employees. When companies try but cannot find the right person for a job opening, they go to these agencies and outsource their work to them so these agencies can find that specific candidate.

I also got in touch with a few recruitment agencies to see if they hade positions similar to what I was looking for, but, usually, I noticed that recruitment agencies do not want to deal with candidates who need sponsorship, so I didn't really have any positive experiences with them. However, I would still suggest you get in touch with a couple of different agencies just to keep your options open because you never know where opportunities can come from.

Also, keep in mind that recruiting agencies generally hire two types of employees: contract employees and full-time employees. A contract employee is someone who is hired for a special project. For example, it can be for three months, six months, or nine months. An employee would go on maternity leave and the company may need someone to cover her position, so it hires a contract worker for a few months. The contract employee works only for the duration of the contract, so this type of employment is only for a certain amount of time. On the other hand, a full-time employee is someone who works until he or she quits that job or until he or she gets laid off. There is no duration for full-time employees.

Sometimes employers hire candidates as contract employees to try their performance in the workplace, and after the contract period ends, the employer can extend the candidate a full-time offer. I know some international students who were hired as contract employees for their OPT periods and then they got extended full-time employment offers with H-1B sponsorships. However, this is a riskier path to take because there is no guarantee that the employer will extend you a full-time job offer and sponsor you at the end of your OPT period.

3 WRITE THE PERFECT RESUME AND COVER LETTER

So far, you have learned your work-authorization rights and the hiring culture in the United States. Now it is time to learn the best way to document your knowledge and experience so you can start applying for jobs. At the end of this chapter, you should be able to put together your power resume and cover letter and get noticed quickly by employers.

What is a resume?
A resume is a document that lists your experience and skills for a job or for whatever you are applying for.

Some countries call this document a CV instead of a resume. For example, in my country, Turkey, everyone uses the CV format and I didn't know what a resume was before coming to the United States. However, I quickly discovered that they both serve the same purpose and the only difference between a CV and a resume is their length. A resume is usually one or two pages long at the most. I really recommend that recent college graduates have a resume that's only one page long.

A CV, on the other hand, can be more than two pages. CV stands for Curriculum Vitae and it's a longer version of the resume. A CV is generally used in the United States by academicians. For example, if you hold a PhD and you've published many books or journal articles, then you usually have a CV because you have more credentials to list.

As mentioned above, in some other countries a CV is more commonly used, and it's usually four or five pages long, but in the United States, the format for nonacademic jobs is one page and it's called a resume.

I will give you an example to illustrate why you need to have a one-page resume as a recent college graduate. When I was interviewing with a candidate in my current company, I noticed that she was very well prepared for the interview. She was good at identifying what the company is doing, who our clients are, and what types of solutions we offer.

She really grabbed all the information that she could about the company from our website, and her skills matched the job role, but she had a three-page resume. She used the resume format of the country that she is from and she didn't follow the US resume standards. In my opinion, this was inappropriate.

At the end of her interview sessions, we got together to talk about her, to decide if we were going to hire her or not. My coworkers also mentioned that she had a three-page resume and all of them cited this as a negative for her. Fortunately, she had lots of positives. She was very well prepared for the interview and she had the right skills for that job, so she was hired.

You may not be as lucky as she was, tough. Your resume may not even pass from the HR department to the hiring managers. Therefore, in order to avoid a negative situation, you should always have a one-page resume if you are looking for an entry-level job. It's not appropriate to use the same resume that you are using in your own country. Remember, you are looking for a job in the United States and not in your own country, so you should follow US resume standards. If we had mixed opinions about hiring the woman mentioned above, maybe she wouldn't have been hired. Thus, don't jeopardize your chances of getting hired by using the wrong resume format.

The reason you should have a one-page resume is that recruiters look at so many resumes in a day that they would like to see your education and experience as fast as they can. Generally, they spend between thirty seconds and one minute on one resume. Therefore, your credentials should be listed in a concise manner.

Let's take a look at the most frequently asked resume questions by students. By following the tips listed in this chapter, you should start putting together your power resume or edit your resume, if you already have one, to make it stand out.

1) How do I write a resume?
There are lots of templates on the web for writing great resumes. You can go to any search engine and type, "how do I write a resume?" or "sample resume" or "resume templates." You can download the resume template you like and start filling it up with your own information.

If you have trouble pulling out information, you can go to your school's career services office and the counselors there can give you a resume template. Another option is to ask your friends who have graduated or who have a one-page US-format resume and they can send you their template so you can fill it with your own data.

2) What type of resume is ideal?
There is no ideal type of resume. It depends on how you want to list your information and the format with which you are comfortable. However, the most common way I have seen is to list information chronologically and start with your educational experience or work experience and list the most relevant data you want to include, starting with the most recent date.

3) What is the most important part of a resume?
In my experience, I found that the most important part of a resume is your work experience. The second most important part is educational experience, but if you don't have much work experience, don't worry. You can list your educational experience first and then list your summer internships or your school projects as your work experience.

For example, if you did a project for a company for a consulting class or for another type of class, you can list it under work experience. In your resume, you can also list the courses you studied toward your degree if you think those courses are related to the skills that employers are looking for. If you are looking for highly technical positions, listing your technical courses might be a good idea.

4) What should I put into my resume?
As mentioned above, you should definitely put your educational experience, work experience, and your special skills on your resume. For example, if you have special computer skills, such as programming in Java or using Photoshop, you should list those under your computer skills section.

You can also list many other things in your resume. For example, if you graduated with honors or if you were on the dean's list for excellent academic grades or if you are part of a swimming team and you won a swim race, you should also list those achievements in your resume.

5) Should I put personal information, such as hobbies and interests, in my resume?

Yes, you can put your hobbies and interests at the end of your resume if you have enough space in your one page. This shows potential employers that you're not only working and studying but you're interested in other things as well.

For example, if you are in a tennis club or you are good at painting or you are a good photographer, you can list those kinds of hobbies and interests in your resume.

6) What is not appropriate to list in your resume?

You should never list in your resume personal information such as your age, your political views, salary information, and reason for termination from previous jobs.

I know in some other countries it is common to list age and gender in your resume, but in the United States never list your age or gender.

7) Why do I need a summary section in my resume?

I recommend that everyone put a summary section at the beginning of your resume and put key words in that section, because when HR people are looking for specific skills, they usually use key words.

For example, if they are looking for someone specialized in data analysis, they use "data analysis" as a key word and type it into their candidate database or LinkedIn or wherever they are pulling resumes from. If they are looking for someone who knows about Internet marketing, they may use Google AdWords or Google Analytics as their key words. They use specific key words to pull up resumes as a faster way to identify the potential candidates for their open positions.

I certainly recommend putting a summary section in your resume and list as many key words as you can in that section to have more visibility.

8) Should I have someone review my resume before sending it off?

Yes, you should have someone review your resume before sending it off. It's very important to have someone else look at it because that person can identify mistakes you may have missed, point out missing items you forgot to add, or help you to edit it.

Remember, a resume is a live document, so it should always be updated and edited every couple of months as you gain new knowledge and work experience.

9) Who can review my resume?

Your school's career services counselors can review your resume. If you don't have career services in your school, then you can ask an employed friend to review it for you.

If you know someone working in HR, you should ask him or her to review your resume. Also you can have headhunters or HR agencies review your resume for you before sending it off to their clients and to other employers. You can also ask them for their opinion about your resume since they are used to seeing many such documents and can help you refine yours.

10) What are the most common mistakes made in resumes?

Usually, punctuation and grammar mistakes are the most common resume mistakes made, and you can avoid these errors by simply doing a spell-check in Word.

Some people never use action verbs in their resumes, so that's another big mistake. You should always use action verbs such as analyzed, built, developed, processed, prepared, etc. You can find a list of the most powerful action verbs by typing "most powerful resume action verbs" into any Internet search engine.

Another common mistake is that some people go on too long or go too short on a subject. You should always find the right balance in listing your information.

That is the end of most frequently asked resume questions. Now, I want everyone to start putting together your power resumes according to the tips explained so far. If you already have a resume, that is great, you can quickly edit it using the tips mentioned so far.

After you finish preparing your power resume, you can start reading the rest of the chapter to learn how to put together a great cover letter.

What is a cover letter?
A cover letter is a document sent along with your resume to provide additional information on your skills and experience.

You should use a cover letter whenever you apply for a job. Usually, companies ask you to also send a cover letter in addition to your resume so they can have a better idea about your skills and experience as well as what you are looking for and what values you can bring to the company.

A cover letter is usually three paragraphs. The first is an opening paragraph in which you introduce yourself and state why you are applying for this position.

The second paragraph is the body of the letter, and it is the most important part of a cover letter. This paragraph lists your experience related to the job you are applying for, why you think you're a good candidate for that position, and what values you can bring to the company.

The third, closing paragraph is where you give the reader a call to action. You state your phone number and e-mail address so the person reading the letter can follow up with you. Keep in mind that a great cover letter is usually less than one page.

Now that we know what a cover letter is and how to write a great cover letter, let's look at some frequently asked questions by students about writing cover letters.

1) Where can I find templates for writing a cover letter?
If you go to a search engine and search for cover letter samples, I am sure you will find many different types of cover letter templates. You can also go to your school's career office and ask the staff for a sample cover letter. Another option is asking friends who have written cover letters before for samples.

2) Should I have a different cover letter for each application?
Yes, absolutely. You should always have a different cover letter for each application. You shouldn't be generic. You should be very specific about the job you are applying for to show that you are a good fit for that position; that you are truly interested in working in that position; and that you will bring more experience to that company because employers are looking for what values you can bring to their company. You can certainly have a general cover letter template, but I recommend that you edit that template for each position you are applying for to tailor it for that position.

Oktay Sekercisoy of Binghamton University's international programs staff says that "you have to adjust your own skills. It's a good idea to look at the online sources to build your resume and cover letter, but at the same time you have to adjust your cover letter and resume based on the needs of that specific job. The mistake that I'm seeing is that students are using the exact same resume and cover letter for all the job applications, which is a big no-no. Don't do that."

He also shares with us a story regarding a candidate who applied for a position in his office. "The person who applied to our office was denied, with good qualifications, because she did not change the address and the organization in her cover letter. She applied to another company and she sent the same letter to us without changing the name of the organization."

This is one of the most common mistakes made by job seekers. They usually send out so many applications that sometimes they forget to update their cover letters according to the position that they are applying for. Always have a final check of your applications before hitting the send button.

3)   Should I send a cover letter with each application?
If you can, yes, you should. I recommend that you send a cover letter with each application so that you can show you are truly interested in that position.

4)   What are the biggest mistakes made in writing a cover letter?
Making a cover letter generic is the biggest mistake because most job seekers usually prepare one cover letter and send it off with every job application.

You should make your cover letter very specific to the job description. Also, a cover letter shouldn't be too long or too short—you should find the appropriate size.

That is all I want to share with you regarding writing a great cover letter. Now, it is your turn to take action and prepare your own cover letter template. After you finish preparing your template, please continue reading the next chapter.

4 JOB-SEARCH PROCESS

In the previous chapters, you learned about your work-authorization rights in the United States and the US hiring culture, and, hopefully, you have put together a great resume and a cover letter. Now, it is time to actually start your job search.

At the beginning of my senior year as an undergraduate at Binghamton University, I absolutely had no idea about where to start my job search. Therefore, I decided to start from the closest place to me, which was my school. I started going to conferences and information sessions held at my school in order to get better prepared for my job search.

Lucy Amello of Bentley University thinks that "students definitely need to get involved quicker. They need to participate in our programs, especially if it involves alumni or if we're bringing employers to speak to them. They also need to participate in mock interviews and career path sessions."

Usually, most schools have a career services office and students can consult with career advisors. Make sure to take the time to speak with them, ask questions, and take advantage of available resources. They are there to help you.

They want you to succeed so they can be successful in what they are doing as well. It is a win-win situation for everybody. Therefore, in addition to reading this book, you should also speak with your career counselor and go to conferences and seminars held in your school so as to be better prepared for your job search.

Moreover, you should attend as many information sessions held by employers as you can because these events give you the chance to meet with recruiters face-to-face. You should ask recruiters questions and let them know what position you are interested in and why you are a good fit for that position. Afterward, you should connect with them on LinkedIn or follow up with an e-mail. This helps the recruiter to remember you, as well as making you stand out from the rest of the applicants, thus increasing your chances of getting invited for an interview.

Information sessions are also a great way to learn more about corporations. If you are not sure what you want to do or where you want to work, speaking with employees of specific companies might help you identify your potential employers and what kind of job you want to do.

I noticed that one of the biggest concerns of students is matching their major and what they have learned in school with the corporate job postings. In order to solve this problem, first, you should decide what you want to do. For example, if you are studying finance, you should decide if you want to work in a bank, in the finance department of a corporation, or in some other entity. Let's say you have decided that you want to work in a bank. Then, you should search what kinds of entry-level jobs banks are posting and what skills they are looking for. Finally, to stand out from the rest of the applicants, you should tailor your resume and cover letter to those jobs that you have decided to apply for.

To illustrate my point, let me cite an example from my own experience. I studied information systems (IT) as an undergraduate. I knew that I didn't want to be a software engineer and I knew that I wanted to work in a position where I could also learn about general business and not only IT, so I decided to apply to IT advisory and consulting companies. First, I decided on the companies that I want to apply to and then looked at those companies to see what positions they were hiring for. As you can see, I targeted a specific group of companies and a specific group of positions to apply for. Finally, I tailored my resume accordingly and applied.

Michael Miller of Culture Adapt says that "if you're too scattered and you're only looking for a job to get an H-1B visa and stay here, then, you're going to be applying all over the place and you're going to fail essentially." Lucy Amello of Bentley University agrees that international students need to be focused on what they're looking for. As you can see, it is always better to be focused rather than applying everywhere generically. Remember, being generic doesn't make you stand out from the rest of the people! Therefore, define your goal and work toward it.

Companies post jobs anywhere nowadays, but if you are not sure what you want to do, I recommend that you first start looking at the job postings on your school's recruiting website because that's where companies usually post entry-level jobs. Then look at the job postings on LinkedIn, Monster.com, or on any other job-search website to see what employers are looking for in an entry-level hire and if you are interested in any of them. Afterward, you can define your goal and start working to achieve it, which is getting hired.

Also, if you took classes about a very specific subject or if you know a specific software program, you can filter the job postings according to those skills and see if employers are looking for those skills. If they are looking for those skills and you want to work in a position where you can apply them, there you go, you have a match! You have identified your goal so you can start working to achieve it.

Keep in mind that as an international student, you can work only in jobs related to your major. This is required so as not to jeopardize your OPT status. For example, you cannot work in a job related to accounting if you studied engineering. Thus, only apply for jobs related to your major. Also, you should start the job-search process as early as possible. For example, if you are a senior and you are graduating in May, you should start looking for a full-time position from the start of the fall semester. You should start in September or October at the latest. Starting early is always better than starting late.

Oktay Sekercisoy of Binghamton University agrees that international students should start looking for a job very early. "They should start thinking about job prospects and possibilities while they are in their sophomore or junior years. It takes time to build the network and build the information network that they will need."

Michael Miller of Culture Adapt shares with us a story that all international students should take lessons from. "Three of my previous interns really wanted to work in the United States and they, like a lot of other students, waited until they graduated to even look for a job. They had two months to look for it and they didn't realize how hard it was going to be. Two out of three of them ended up going back home. They both have jobs in other countries now. They're all very smart people, but they just didn't understand how hard the process would be here and the limited number of visas."

Think of the job-search process as a four-credit course. You should put as much time and effort into the job-search process as you are putting into a four-credit course. Thus, if you start early, you can manage your time wisely. The number one reason international students cannot find a job in the United States is that they don't put enough effort into this process. They apply to companies without defining their end goals, without tailoring themselves for the job opening and without trying to meet recruiters to make themselves stand out from their peers. When they are not invited for an interview by the companies they applied to, they give up and complain that finding a job in the United States is very difficult. If you really put in enough effort and define a strategy for yourself, finding a job in the United States is not as difficult as you think. I had three sponsored job offers in my hand when I was graduating with my MBA. Why? I was focused, I defined my end goals, and I took my steps accordingly. There is no reason why you cannot do the same as well.

Michael Miller of Culture Adapt says that "some people understand the job-search process, but most people from my experience don't understand the amount of time you need to put into it and they don't prioritize it."

Lucy Amello of Bentley University also thinks that "there are some international students who are very dedicated to their job search and very focused and there are international students who really don't do all the things that they're supposed to do, including market research, being focused, participating in events, and those are the ones who all of a sudden wake up three or four months before graduation and say, 'Oh my God, I have to go back now because I don't have a job.' "

It really depends on you. If you put enough time and effort into your job search and do everything explained in this book, there is no reason you cannot find a sponsored job in the United States.

The importance of internships:
If you started your job-search process late or you couldn't put enough effort into it or your time is running short—for example if you are graduating in May and you're already in April but you don't have any interviews lined up or no one is calling you—then you should start applying to internships. Assuming you get an internship and work for a company for a few months and provide your best performance, then there is a big possibility that at the end of your internship period, you might be offered a fulltime position.

Internships are crucial in your efforts to land a full-time job because you build your skills and gain more experience. Also, you can build your reputation and have references to help you land your full-time sponsored position. You can list your references on LinkedIn and share this information with potential employers and show that you'll bring value to them.

Michael Miller of Culture Adapt says, "I think it is very important to get internships nowadays and its experience, and you can do that right from freshman year. I would definitely suggest to get some internships lined up." Oktay Sekercisoy of Binghamton University also agrees that internships are crucial in landing a full-time position. "One of the issues for any student, but especially for international students, before you graduate, you should have some internship activities on your resume or some professional involvement activities that show your leadership style or your personality, the way that you are."

Maybe corporations think that you are not ready to take the responsibilities of a full-time job yet, and that could be why you are not being called for interviews. However, if you have several internships listed on your resume, you increase your chances of being invited to interviews and finally landing a full-time sponsored position.

If you still have at least a year before you graduate, I recommend that you do at least two internships before your final semester in school. I had several internships listed on my resume during my senior year as an undergraduate. Personally, I didn't want to spend my summers in the United States, so I always returned home during summer breaks and never did an internship in the United States. However, I was still able to get a full-time sponsored job here. Do you know how I did this? I was able to do this because in almost all of my summer internships in my home country, I worked for either American or global corporations. Some of the corporations I interned for in my country included Microsoft, Frito-Lay, and HSBC. Each represents a different industry (because I like exploring new things), but they all have one thing in common. They are global! People know these companies. When recruiters looked at my resume, they recognized these companies and were able to get an idea about my roles and responsibilities during my internship. Therefore, if you cannot find an internship in the United States, do an internship in your home country, but do it for a global corporation, one that other employers will recognize so you increase your chances of being hired as a full-time employee in the United States.

Also, if you can, try to apply for jobs and internships throughout the United States and not just in the area where your school is located, which may not always have the jobs related to your major. For example, if you are studying fashion, then you should probably look for a job in New York because it is the capital of fashion, or if you are studying biology, then you should look for a job around Boston because there are lots of medical companies and research labs around Boston.

The importance of campus involvement:
If you don't have enough time for internships while school is in session, you can try to be more active in your school by

joining student clubs or by doing volunteer work. These are great activities to list on your resume as well as to show employers that you can take initiative in your community.

Oktay Sekercisoy of Binghamton University shares a story about a student he knew: "We had a student who was hired by Goldman Sachs in her first semester as a senior-year student. She was going to graduate in May, but in October she was already hired by Goldman Sachs. She was hired seven months prior to her graduation.

What she did was she was well involved on our campus. She attended a German club. She spoke Turkish and English. At the same time, she took a German course and attended the German club and she was very active on campus, although she was an international student.

She made friends with other American students and she volunteered in some other projects that were a resume builder for her. When she went to the job fair in September, she was not afraid to talk and she presented herself. She presented her resume and her credentials. Actually I met her that day. She looked so professional from her outfit, from her hair, everything.

Her resume was perfect. It was filled with volunteer activities, projects that she was involved in, and she listed some courses that were relevant to the job that Goldman Sachs was looking for. I think that was a great success story. What she did was that in her resume on the top she highlighted her skills. She did not just focus on her technical skills. She focused on her skills from an international perspective. For example, she put a sentence that living in two different countries contributed to her adaptability and adaptability to change.

She was highlighting that being an international student helped her personally to be able to adapt to change very easily. That was something that was unique for an international student that an American student who never left the country might have not provided to that organization.

She looked at her strengths and she highlighted her strengths in the resume, in her application."

In my opinion, this is a great success story, and there is no reason you cannot have a similar story as well. Build your resume early on either through internships, student clubs, or volunteer activities. These will help you stand out from the crowd and present yourself as a unique candidate for any job.

Keep track of all the applications submitted:

It is better to track all the applications you submitted so that you don't forget and reapply to companies that you have already contacted. But sometimes it's very difficult to keep track of where you apply, especially if you're a senior and you're applying to multiple positions a day. However, it's very useful to track who called you or who responded to your applications or inquiries so that you can always follow up if you didn't hear back from someone that you expected to hear from. You can always look up the document you created and follow up with people from whom you expect to hear. I didn't do this, but I know people who did it and it is actually very handy.

There are situations where you apply to a company and you hear back very quickly. Potential employers may respond in a week or two if you met with them at a job fair or at a networking event, but sometimes you don't hear back for months and sometimes you just get a rejection letter. You never know what is going to happen. Let me tell you this story. During my job search, I attended as many career fairs and met as many employers as I could. I met so many employers that it was very hard for me to keep track of them and remember them unless they contacted me within a month. I gave my resume to my current employer, Merkle Inc., at a career fair on campus in October. When someone from Merkle called me for an initial phone interview, I couldn't remember when or how I met with the company's representatives, so I asked. The interviewer explained to me that his supervisor had met with me at a campus fair on October and was very impressed. He then told me that they would like to invite me to their office for a day-long interview session. Do you know what is strange about this story? They called me in March! Yes, five months after I met with them! I was very impressed that they actually kept my resume for five months and still remembered me. I had even forgotten that I applied to that company. However, if I had kept an Excel spreadsheet to track my applications, figuring out when and how I applied to that company would have been much easier.

Online job applications:
If you only apply for jobs online directly through career websites, there is a high possibility that your resume would get lost in the shuffle. HR personnel usually get so many resumes in a day that they cannot keep track of all the resumes that they get.

Moreover, they usually give preference to referrals or to the people they met at career fairs or at networking events. By the time they get to the resumes submitted through career websites, most likely they have already identified and found a good number of potential candidates, so they don't need to look very carefully at website-generated resumes.

It is always better to find someone working for your target company to refer you to the HR personnel so that your resume can be picked up quickly. Then, if HR thinks you are a good fit for an open position, you would be invited for an interview. It is much faster to be called for an interview if you connect with other people. This is called networking. I will talk about the importance of networking in the next chapter.

Also, keep in mind that connecting with the hiring manager is much better than connecting with the HR personnel because hiring managers know what skills they want from an employee better than the HR personnel. If the position you are applying for is highly technical, the HR employee may not have the necessary background to identify you as a potential candidate for the position. For example, let's assume you majored in bioinformatics and you have applied for a position related to bioinformatics. If the company's HR employees have no information about bioinformatics, then it's very hard for them to identify you as a good candidate for the position and they may overlook your resume and the skills you have. However, hiring managers know what skills they are looking for, so it's easier for them to identify a good candidate to interview. It's always better to connect with the person that you are going to work with in the future rather than with the HR personnel.

The importance of social media in the job-search process:
You should use LinkedIn for your job search because you can connect with other people very easily on a professional level and you can send messages directly to them. You can also list your knowledge and work experience and apply for other jobs with your LinkedIn profile.

You should also make sure there is nothing inappropriate on your Facebook page and that the page is closed to other people because employers will look you up on social media and on search engines to see what you have posted. Don't forget that they are researching you just as you are researching them.

Best ways to get an interview:
I have mentioned the best ways to get an interview throughout this chapter, but to sum it all up, I recommend

that you go to career fairs and information sessions and meet with recruiters face-to-face. Also, use LinkedIn and try to connect with people who are already employed at the company you are planning to apply to and have them refer you to their HR department.

You need to make an impression on the employers and show that you are going to bring value to their organizations. Therefore, it is important to meet with them face-to-face so you can explain easily why you want to work for them and why you are a good fit for the position you are interested in. This enables you to make a first connection with them, and it increases your chances of being invited for an interview.

Now, let's take a look at the most frequently asked questions by international students about the job-search process in the United States:

1) Is it easy to find a job as an international student?
I want to answer this question by quoting one of the students who took my international student survey. Omar thinks that "the question is not a matter of difficulty, but rather qualifications of the job seeker. Of course it will be a challenge, due to the available competition. However, if the person is the shiny crayon in the box, he/she will be able to find a job. Beyond this point, it is a question if the firm is willing to sponsor the international student; that is another challenge. Yet again, if that student is valuable and is a great asset to have, the employer might not have a problem with that."

Wendy D'Ambrose, Director of Graduate Career Services at Bentley University, echoes that sentiment, pointing out that "students have to remember that they're in a situation where they are selling, the employer is buying, so they have to meet the employer's needs. It's not about what the student wants only. It's about what value can I give to this employer. Why should the employer go the extra bit to sponsor me?"

You have to convince employers that you are better suited for that job compared with your domestic peers and that you will bring more value to their organizations so they can pay the required sponsoring fees to hire you.

2)   What steps do I need to take to find a job in the United States?

Finding a job in the United States is a process, and there are many different steps involved in this process, such as knowing the hiring culture, having a great resume, knowing how to network, and knowing how to interview. If you play the game right, then you have better chances of winning it.

3)   Do I need to study in the United States first to be eligible to work there?

No, if you already have an undergraduate degree in another country and you can find an employer who will sponsor you, then you don't need a separate degree from a US college or university. I have friends who studied computer science in Turkey and came to the United States for summer vacation for two months to visit their friend and found a job as Java programmers through that friend. Also, if you are already working for a global corporation in your country and that corporation has operations in the United States, you can come here to work with an L-1 visa. When I was working at KPMG LLP, I had a coworker from Germany who originally worked at KPMG LLP's Germany office but came to work at the New York office with an L-1 visa. However, these cases are rare and studying in the United States and having a US college degree always increases your chances of being hired there.

4)   Why do companies want to hire international students?

Companies hire international students because sometimes they cannot find some of the skills that they are looking for among the domestic students. Therefore, they hire international students to fill that skills gap.

For example, statistics show that there aren't many domestic computer science students studying programming in Java. Consequently, employers looking to hire an entry-level Java programmer would have difficulty finding enough qualified candidates to fill those jobs. Therefore, in order not to limit their options, employers hire international students who can program in Java.

Companies usually want to hire the best person for a position, so that's why they keep their options open.

Below are the opinions of people who are helping international students professionally:

Michael Miller, president of Culture Adapt:
"Some companies love diversity and understand that diverse backgrounds and thoughts are going to provide you with innovation and better results overall. Other companies think, 'I'm going to have to train this person. They're not going to understand the business culture. This is tougher. I don't want to deal with the hassle of immigration.' "

Oktay Sekercisoy, director for International Partnership Development at Binghamton University:
"It depends on the job characteristics of companies because some companies have specific jobs that they are really looking for someone culturally adept and culturally knows the system, the country and the background and all of that.

Some companies might have already experienced hiring international students so they might feel comfortable with the process and they might think that having an international person in their organization might change the operations in terms of bringing new perspectives to their company. They might be more comfortable going through that immigration and paperwork process. They might be more willing to hire international students.

For example, if the company is an auditing company that has only American clients, it might not be beneficial for that company to have international students in the organization, but if the same auditing company has international clients from India, China, or Turkey, or European countries, they might think that having an international person in that organization who might work with international clients would be beneficial for them so it's easy for them to hire international people."

Lucy Amello, associate director of graduate career services at Bentley University:
"I have to say it depends on the industry, on the need and how difficult it is to get employees for that company. For example, if they need special education within the IT world, our Indian students come with so many years of IT experience and then, they add MSIT to their work experience and that makes them very marketable for the IT companies. I think that is the main issue here."

5) Are some jobs more in demand by US employers? What are those?
Yes, absolutely. Jobs that require technical skills, mathematical skills, computer skills, and graphic design skills are in high demand in the United States. Also, many domestic students do not major in those areas, so I personally recommend to many international students to take at least two to three technical and computer programming courses so they can increase their chances of finding a sponsored job in the United States.

Oktay Sekercisoy of Binghamton University thinks that being an international student might be advantageous for you regarding technical jobs, which are related to science, technology, engineering, or math, because some of the countries that send students to the United States for higher education have very strong high school education. On top of that strong high school foundation you already have, you are adding a good college education in the United States. Thus, you might be in an advantageous position compared with domestic students.

6) Why doesn't every US company hire international students?

There is not one right answer for this question. It might be due to many different reasons. For example, some government and defense organizations do not hire international students because they require a security clearance and only US citizens can provide this security clearance to them. Another reason might be budget issues—hiring an international student requires a few extra thousand dollars compared with hiring domestic students, and if a company has tight budget constraints, it might not be able to hire international students. Another reason might be the policies that a company has. If a company is global and it has a location in your home country, it might want to hire you for that location due to its hiring policies.

Another reason might be that they don't know whether they can hire international students. Lucy Amello of Bentley University thinks "recruiters are changing very often these days and the education is not there anymore as far as how the entire process works. You can't sponsor someone based on just liking the person. It has to be based on a need of that specific skill and those are the things that I think recruiters have to be educated with more."

Oktay Sekercisoy of Binghamton University thinks that employers can have many different reasons for not hiring international students. "One reason might be the fact that they think US citizens or American students will take less time to train. As I said, one might be because of the job characteristics. The other one might be because they are not familiar with the immigration system and they might think that it will be a longer process and difficult process to hire international students and they might not have a department in their organization to do that paperwork or follow on these requirements.

Instead if there's an equally trained and well-educated American person, they might just go and hire that person without any kind of process or paperwork."

7) How do I find a list of companies sponsoring H-1B visas so I can apply only to those companies?

The best way to find the list of companies sponsoring H-1B is asking them. You can ask in the interviews or you can go to your school's career office and career counselors there can tell you which companies offer H-1B sponsorships. Usually, schools keep track of which employers hired international students in the previous years. You can also ask someone working for the company you are interested in or who may know a HR employee working for that company.

You can also search the companies on the Internet. You can go to www.myvisajobs.com and search by company name to see if they have sponsored anyone in the previous years.

8) What if the company I want to apply to doesn't sponsorH-1B visas?

You can offer to work for the company with your OPT authorization for a year so that if it likes your performance and wants to keep you, it can sponsor you for an H-1B visa.

You can try to negotiate with the company by saying, "I really want to work in this position. Let me work with my OPT for one year and if you are happy with my performance, you can sponsor me next year so I can keep working for you."

You can also try to educate the employers that sponsoring is not as complicated as they think. Wendy D'Ambrose of Bentley University says that "some companies have no idea how this all works because sponsorship is scary to them. They think it's costly. They think it's time consuming. They're more afraid of it than against it in my opinion." If you explain to companies how the process works, they may change their opinions on sponsoring you for an H-1B visa.

If they let you work with your OPT authorization but cannot sponsor you for an H-1B visa, then you need to stop working for them once your OPT authorization ends. You can still try to negotiate with them, but if they don't have the budget for it or if they have strict rules against sponsoring international students, then you should try to look for other jobs that have better sponsorship opportunities.

5 THE IMPORTANCE OF NETWORKING

In the previous chapters, you learned your work authorization rights and the hiring culture in the United States. You have put together a great resume and a cover letter, and you have started searching for jobs. Now, it is time to connect with other individuals who can help you get an interview with the corporations that you want to work for. The best way to get these interviews is through networking.

<u>What is networking and why is it important?</u>
Networking is meeting and sharing information with individuals and groups of people in your field of interest. For example, in your case, these people include potential employers, recruiters, head hunters and HR agencies.

Networking is very easy to do if you do it right. You can network pretty much anywhere and with whoever you are interested in networking with. There's no restriction. You can even network when you're riding on the subway. You can start talking with the person you are sitting next to and make a new connection.

Networking is all about meeting with new people and expanding your network. However, it also depends on what you are trying to accomplish by meeting these new people. In your case, it is important to meet the right people to get the interviews you want. In order to meet the right people, you should start going to networking events, such as events related to the industry you are looking to work in or job fairs or information sessions held in your school.

Networking is one of the most crucial steps in finding an H-1B sponsorship job in the United States because it increases your chances of getting hired. It's always better if you meet face-to-face with employers at networking events or job fairs so you can show your personality and mention your experience briefly. As a result, employers have a better idea of who you are, and sometimes they can even do a short interview with you right on the spot to see whether you are the right candidate for that job.

For example, when I attended job fairs and handed out my resume to employers, they asked me questions about my resume and why I was interested in a particular job. As you can see, they were actually holding a mini interview with me so that they could identify if I was a good candidate for that position.

Wendy D'Ambrose of Bentley University's graduate career services shares with us a story about a former student. "I had a student who was at one of our events and was an ambassador to a particular employer. It was an international student. The employer who was recruiting on campus, made it clear that they do not sponsor. The student was fine, gracious, smart, built a relationship, connected. Lo and behold, at the end of the day, the employer was like, "You know? We really do need to talk to you." Long story short, the student is working there now with H-1B sponsorship. You just never know. It goes back to building a relationship.

It goes back to looking for the decision makers. It goes back to being a good sport."

Oktay Sekercisoy of Binghamton University agrees that networking is very important and shares his networking story on how he heard about and applied for his current position. "Of course international students have to focus on finding a job, but at the same time they should focus on building a network. A network of people that can get information to them and at the same time a network of people that can be a reference for them. This network of people might be US citizens in the same class or at the same project. They might go and find a job first and then they can be a lead for international students to find a job.

Personally, I came to the US as an international student and I found my job through my network. Although my job was announced for public, before my job was announced for public I knew that this job was going to open and they were going to hire somebody for this position.

My friends, my network, told me to be on the lookout for a job that's going to open at Binghamton University. The minute the job was opened I applied. I might be the first one that applied to that job. Instead of waiting online or in the newspaper that the job will be announced, your network can tell you the job openings and it will be very helpful."

The importance of networking through LinkedIn:
As I mentioned in the previous chapters, networking through LinkedIn is also important for landing a job, because on LinkedIn potential employers can see your education, skills, and what your previous work experience is. They can also see your references from your previous work experience.

LinkedIn is a great networking tool because it allows you to connect easily with other people on a professional level. You can send a message saying, "I'm interested in working for your company in so and so position. I see that you are already working in that company. Is it OK if I connect with you to ask a few questions about your company?" and maybe your questions might turn into an informational interview.

You never know when and where a job offer is going to come from. In my case, I received one of my job offers after applying for a position that I found through LinkedIn. I applied for the job using my LinkedIn profile and the employer found my skills valuable and called me for an interview.

After my second interview with the company, the hiring manager gave me an offer right on the spot, a response that was even quicker than I expected. Thus, you never know when and where the offers might come from.

How do I become good at networking?
You can only become good at networking by practicing. You should attend as many networking events and talk with as many people as you can. You can start practicing networking in the mirror first by refining your personal pitch. You can go to the mirror and try to talk with yourself for a couple of minutes and figure out the best way of introducing yourself in less than a minute. You can also practice networking while using public transportation. For example, you can try to network in the subway with strangers.

If you are shy and scared of talking with strangers, you can start networking with your peers first. Lucy Amello of Bentley University suggests that students sign up for conversation-partner programs in universities to open up. I also agree that it's always easier to network with your peers in the school. Students are always open to meeting other students and their peers. For example, you can try to meet with other students in your class or in the cafeteria. Oktay

Sekercisoy of Binghamton University suggests that students get involved in their college and join student clubs to network with other students as well as add some valuable activity to their resume.

You can try to network with your classmates and other students first, and then by practicing, as you become better, you can start networking with HR professionals or other employers. I personally recommend you to make a goal for yourself to meet at least one new student every day in your campus. By this way, you will be able to overcome your shyness and become more comfortable meeting new people.

You can also ask other people for help so you can practice networking with them. You can get help from your school as well. You don't need to be alone. I'm sure people will help or they will practice with you if you ask.

Keeping track of all the people you have met:
I highly recommend keeping track of all the people you have met. In order to do this, try to get their business cards when you meet them. If they are on LinkedIn, add them to your contacts, and you can e-mail them or talk with them later when you need to. If they don't use LinkedIn, then keep their business cards or e-mail addresses.

It is a good gesture to follow up with people you have met at networking events. You can send a nice thank-you e-mail saying, "Thank you for our conversation today. It was very nice to meet with you. I hope we keep in touch." That's how easy it is. Afterward, you can save their e-mail addresses to your address book and you can add them on LinkedIn. You can put their business cards in a folder. There are all kind of different ways to keep track of their information.

When you are networking, it is very important to grab the attention of the person you are talking with, as a way to show your skills and values. Therefore, you need to have a great personal elevator pitch. In the rest of the chapter, I will explain how to develop your personal elevator pitch.

<u>What is a personal elevator pitch and how do I develop it?</u>
It's a short summary to define you, to define what you are looking for. You can develop your personal elevator pitch by searching the Internet and looking at examples of how to write a personal pitch. You can ask your school's career office, friends, or other people. For example, if there are people in your family working for global corporations, then you can ask them and get their ideas as well.

The elevator pitch should include who you are, what your work experience is, and why someone should hire you. You should clearly state what you have studied, where you have worked previously, and what you are looking for right at that moment. The elevator pitch shouldn't be long, like a five-minute conversation. It should be thirty to sixty seconds long. It should be very concise.

Drafting a great personal pitch comes with practice. It doesn't happen overnight. You should get help on how to make your personal pitch so you can explain clearly to others your values as well as what you are looking for.

I highly recommend practicing your pitch in the mirror first and then practicing with family members, friends, and advisors to get their feedback and see what they are thinking about your pitch and revise it accordingly.

A personal elevator pitch is a living speech. The things that you want for your career might change eventually, so you should always update your pitch according to what you have done and what you are looking for.

Now, I want you to find a few examples of personal elevator pitches on the Internet using search engines and put together your own elevator pitch. After practicing this pitch in front of the mirror first, practice it with other people.

After you have met with people and networked with them, if you still want to keep in touch with them, you can send them a thank-you letter. In the rest of this chapter, I will explain thank-you letters and why we need to write them.

What is a thank-you letter and why should you send one?

A thank-you letter is a follow-up note that you send to people after you have met or interviewed with them. For example, if you met with a recruiter at a career fair and you are really interested in a particular position and want to get invited for an interview, you should follow up with the recruiter, saying, "I was pleased to meet with you at the job fair today. As a result of our conversation, I learned a lot about the company, and this has increased my interest in working for you." This note will serve to remind the recruiter of you and that you are still interested in the job.

You can also use thank-you letters after an interview to thank the interviewer for taking the time to interview with you.

Sending a thank-you letter shows your interest. It shows that you are interested in that position and in that company. Also, it is a good way of showing your appreciation to the person who took the time to talk with you and meet with you.

Some people think that employers don't read thank-you letters and they, therefore, choose not to send such letters because they think it is a waste of time. You never know if they read these letters or not. Some employers read them, but others don't. However, I know of people who lost job offers just because they didn't send a thank-you letter. In one case, there were only two candidates left for a position and the hiring managers didn't know who to eliminate, and finally somebody said, "This person is not very interested in this position because he didn't send me a thank-you letter. Let's offer the position to the other person who seems more interested, since she followed up with a thank-you letter." Now, do you want to take any risks by not sending a thank-you letter?

Even if the intended recipient doesn't read your thank-you letter, you should always follow up because this shows your interest. Moreover, no one wants to lose a potential offer just because he or she didn't send a thank-you letter, which takes only a few minutes of your time. Therefore, in my opinion, thank-you letters are very important.

How to write a thank-you letter and send it:
A thank-you letter should be very short, about two sentences long. It should show your appreciation to the person who took the time to meet with you or interview with you. It's only about thanking them. A sample thank-you letter would be, "Thank you for taking the time to meet/interview with me. I enjoyed our conversation and learning more about the company and the position. I look forward to hearing back from you soon."

The common way of sending a thank-you letter is through e-mail because it is fast and easy. It doesn't cost anyone any money. I don't recommend sending it through social media platforms, because not everyone looks at these platforms on a day-to-day basis. I also do not recommend sending it through regular mail, because it can get lost and regular mail takes a few days to arrive. E-mail is easy and fast, so it is best to send it through e-mail.

6 GOT THE INTERVIEW! NOW WHAT?

In the previous chapters, you learned your work-authorization rights and the recruiting culture in the United States. You have also put together a great resume and a cover letter, you have started searching for jobs, and you have expanded your network and followed up with the individuals you have met. If you have done correctly everything mentioned up to this chapter, most probably you should have been invited to a couple of different interviews. Now, we will learn how to ace those interviews so you will get the offer you are dreaming of.

First, let's discuss the types of interviews common in the United States. There are several different types of interview you are likely to go through: phone interview, technical interview, behavioral interview, case interview, and presentation interview. There may be other kinds of interviews as well, but these are the most common. In this chapter, I will mainly talk about behavioral interviews and explain how to address some of the most frequently asked questions during those interviews.

Interview types:

1) Behavioral interview:

A behavioral interview is an interview where employers try to find out about your personality, your character, and your soft skills to see if you are a good fit for the position and the company culture. The interview focuses on experience, behaviors, knowledge, skills, and abilities that are related to the job. In this type of interview, you should respond to questions by giving examples from your previous work experience, activities, hobbies, volunteer work, or school projects.

2) Technical interview:

A technical interview evaluates your technical skills related to the job, such as your computer skills or your design skills. This type of interview is generally conducted by someone working in a similar position or by someone who is knowledgeable in what is needed for that position and can assess your technical abilities.

3) Case interview:

A case interview generally includes a business case that the interviewer or someone else from the company has worked on in real life. This business case usually involves a problem or a challenge that needs to be resolved. In this type of interview, generally employers want to see how you work on a problem and what steps you take to get to the solution.

4) Mock interview:

A mock interview is a preparation interview for the real one. Usually, a school's career services office conducts a mock interview with you so that you can get used to interviewing and become better prepared for your real interview.

A mock interview is a great way to get feedback regarding your interviewing skills. "Mock interviews are great resources if you are an international student because at the end of that interview you get the feedback about how you answered questions and what you need to improve," Oktay Sekercisoy of Binghamton University.

5) On-campus interview:
An on-campus interview is one conducted on campus by employers. It's only for the students of the school where the interview is taking place. In this case, there is a very high possibility that you will do at least one on-campus interview if you start your job-search process early.

It's actually more advantageous to do on-campus interviews. As I noticed, since students are in a place that they already know, they generally feel more comfortable during on-campus interviews than when they go to the offices of the companies to interview.

Also, some companies hold information sessions on campus before the interviews to give you an idea about their culture and what they are looking for in the candidates. Therefore, to get ready for your interview, it is best to attend those sessions, meet with the people who are going to interview you, and ask questions about the company, the job role, and what they are typically looking for in their new hires.

So far in this chapter, you have learned the most common types of interviews. Now, it is time to move on to learning about how to acquire great interview skills and, as a result, get the offer you want. International students usually have many questions about interviewing. Therefore, I would like to continue this chapter by answering the most frequently asked questions by international students. I will also explain how to address the most common questions asked by employers during interviews.

<u>Most common questions about interviews:</u>

1)   How long is a typical interview?
A typical interview usually lasts a half an hour. You usually interview with one person for thirty minutes and then maybe interview with another person back-to-back for another thirty minutes. However, if you are scheduled to have back-to-back interviews with multiple people in the same organization, the sessions can last anywhere from half an hour to a few hours.

2)   How do I prepare for an interview?
The best way to prepare for an interview is by practicing. You should practice, practice, practice. When I was a senior in college, I practiced with my roommate. I gave her questions that I got from the school's career services office and from the Internet and asked her to interview me. I stayed in a four-room suite with eight people living in it, so I asked a different roommate each time I wanted to practice interviewing. This approach worked for me and helped me to land my first full-time position at KPMG LLP's New York office. I recommend that you use a similar approach and practice interviewing with whoever you can find.

3)   How do I become good at interviewing?
As I explained in my answer to the previous question, you can only become good at interviewing by practicing. You should practice with anyone you can find, such as family members, your school's career office personnel, professors, or friends.

I did at least twenty interviews during the last year of my MBA studies, and the more you interview the better you become. I took every single interview opportunity I was given even if it was just an informational interview and not a real job interview. Why? Because you only get better at interviewing if you practice! As a result, I got three H-1B sponsorship job offers from three great companies. I am sure many of you are wondering how I found twenty interview opportunities when most people find only a handful. If you are reading this chapter and still do not know the answer to this question, I recommend you go back to the previous chapter, The Importance of Networking, and read it once more.

4) What information do I need to know about the company before the interview?

You should go to the company's website and grab as much information as you can from there. Most companies have a website nowadays so you can easily learn what their business is about, who their clients are, and what their departments are, such as IT, marketing, finance, etc. Learn as much as you can about that company before going to the interview.

5) How many interviews do I need to do before getting hired?

There is not one right answer for this question. It really depends on the company. Some companies conduct only two interviews: a phone interview and a behavioral interview. On the other hand, some companies can conduct as many as six or more interviews. It really depends on the company. If you ask companies about their hiring process, they will probably tell you how many interviews they conduct before giving out a job offer.

6) What are the most common interview questions and how do I answer them correctly?

The most common interview question that I got was, "Tell me about yourself." Every interviewer asks this question, and it's the first question that you generally get and the most important question in my opinion because if you cannot grab the interviewer's attention with your response to this question, there is a high possibility that you will not get a job offer.

You should answer this question not only in a concise manner but also in a way that will impress the interviewer so he or she would like to learn more about you. You should list your previous work experience and your education, but by highlighting your success stories along the way. For example, I would answer this question like this: I graduated with my bachelor of science degree with <u>honors</u> from the dual-diploma program of SUNY Binghamton and Istanbul Technical University in Turkey majoring in information systems. I <u>fulfilled both schools' requirements in four years</u> in order to <u>get a bachelor of science degree from each school</u>. After graduating, I started working at KPMG LLP's New York City office as an IT advisory associate. While working at KPMG LLP, one of my coworkers decided to leave the company and <u>I took over her responsibilities in addition to my responsibilities</u> to meet project deadlines. After working in this position for a year, I decided to go for my MBA at Bentley University <u>with a scholarship</u>. After graduating from Bentley University's MBA program <u>with distinction,</u> I started working at Merkle Inc. as a business systems analyst.

As you can see from the underlined text, I am not only listing my education and work experience, but I am also highlighting my success stories to impress the interviewer. You don't need to finish school with a cum laude degree, but I am sure everyone has at least one educational or professional success story that he or she is proud of and would like to share with other people. The key is finding that success story and sharing it with employers.

Now, I need you to write the first draft of your answer to this question. Note that this will not be your final answer. You should practice for this question as much as you can with your school's career services professionals, with friends, or with professors and get feedback from them to revise it and finally make it perfect.

The second most frequently asked question by employers is, "What values are you going to bring to us?." I noticed that most students answer this question by stating what they want to do in their careers and how they would like to proceed and what they want to learn, but no one answers the real question of what they are actually bringing to the company. Don't make this mistake.

In order to answer this question, you should thoroughly know the company you are interviewing with in addition to the job role you are interviewing for. You should match your education, your skills, and your previous work experience with the job description and mention that you already have some experience in that field so you can learn and help them faster. Also, you should match your personal skills with the company's culture and show that you will fit into the culture well. Moreover, since you are from another country, you can tell them you will bring diversity to their business and you will be able to approach situations from a different point of view.

These were the two most popular questions asked during my interviews. For other questions, you can search the Internet and try to find out what the most common interview questions are. You can use any search engine or you can go to the career websites of companies and they usually have questions that they ask their candidates. Especially, if you look at the websites of global enterprises, under their college-recruiting section, they usually post the questions they generally ask the college hires. I highly recommend printing those questions and studying for them with your college's career services counselor.

7) Where can I find a list of interview questions that companies usually ask recent college grads?

As mentioned above, you can get a list of popular interview questions from your school's career services center or from the Internet. The best place to look for this information on the Internet is the websites of global enterprises, under their college-recruiting section.

8) How do I know my selling points in an interview?

First of all, you should prepare for an interview. If you already studied the company and the job role, you should match whatever is on your resume and whatever knowledge you have with that specific job role and try to emphasize that in the interview.

For example, if the company is looking for someone with database knowledge, then you should emphasize what databases courses you took in college or what database programming language you know or what database work you did for other companies.

During your interview, you should emphasize whatever the employer is looking for so that you can show that you are the ideal fit for the position. Remember, you have to convince employers that you are better compared with your domestic peers and that you will bring more value to their organization so they can pay the required sponsoring fees to hire you.

9) How do I turn my disadvantages into advantages during an interview?

Usually, international students think that it's a disadvantage that they come from another country, and that is not true. Of the students I surveyed, 45 percent said that being from another country is a disadvantage in trying to find a job in the United States, 27 percent said it is an advantage, and the rest were not sure.

Most companies value diverse hires. You can say, "I'm an international student. I worked in country XYZ for two years before coming to the United States for my masters' degree. Therefore, I will bring a different point of view to your company because I have overseas working experience." This is a very positive experience for many employers.

Michael Miller of Culture Adapt says, "I think that people coming from another country have a really good set of skills. You're bilingual automatically, which is well and above most Americans. A lot of companies really value that diverse background."

Wendy D'Ambrose of Bentley University says that "being from another country is an advantage because it adds diversity. It adds interest and you have different people working together. It kind of really stands for what America is all about, if you have a diverse company."

As you can see, contrary to what many students think, being from another country is an advantage in the US job market.

Another piece of advice on turning your perceived disadvantages into advantages is that if the interviewer asks you a question about something that you have no experience with, don't just say no and become quiet. Instead, try to explain why you don't have any experience with it and show that you are very open to learning more about it. For example, in my senior year as an undergraduate, during one of my interviews with an audit and advisory company, I was asked if I ever had any experience with SOX (Sarbanes-Oxley Act). Obviously, SOX is an American federal law and I am from Turkey and until then, all my internships had been in Turkey. However, I didn't just say no and leave it at that. I said, "Although I never had any experience with SOX, because I am from Turkey and we don't have anything similar to SOX in place, I know what it is," and I explained to him what it is and the interviewer seemed satisfied with my answer. So instead of simply saying, "No, I don't have any experience," I showed him that I was interested in the topic and I knew what SOX is and also explained to him why I didn't have any experience with it.

Don't forget you can only turn your disadvantages into advantages by knowing how to package them correctly during interviews.

10) What do employers look for in candidates in an interview?
They usually look for what value the candidate is going to bring to their organization. Although they would like to hear what you are interested in doing, they are generally looking for what values you can bring to them.

One of the most common mistakes made in interviews is that candidates always talk about their interests. They say, "I want to learn about this, do that, learn about this and build my career about that." It's good that you have a career plan for yourself and you are showing that you're interested in the position and it fits into your career goals. Nevertheless, rather than emphasizing your career aspirations, you should always emphasize your professional experience, your skills, and what you are going to bring to an organization with your background.

11) What do employers want to hear in an interview?
They want to hear about your success stories, your

abilities, your values, and what you can do to make their company better.

Sometimes they even want to hear about your personal skills. For example, if you are the designated event organizer among your friends, you may say, "I'm a great event organizer. I always organize events among my friends, so I will use this approach to organize events for the team and make the team bond together better." This is a great way to show your soft skills.

12) Should I ask questions in an interview?

Yes, you should ask questions in an interview. You should always study the company and write down a few questions that you want to ask to the interviewer. These can be specific questions, such as the projects the company is working on or its clients. Otherwise, the questions can also be general, such as the benefits the company offers or training opportunities within the company. No matter what type of questions you ask, you should always ask questions in an interview. Evidently, the more specific questions you ask, the more interested you seem in the company and the position.

13) What types of questions should I ask in an interview?

You can ask either general or specific questions. However, it is better if you ask specific questions about the company and the job role. For example, you can ask the following questions: "What are my job responsibilities going to be?" "If I am hired for this position, what am I going to do day to day?" "Who am I going to report to?"

Some people ask questions that are too general during interviews. For example, "How many holidays do you give to your employees in a year?" You shouldn't ask a general question like this because it looks as if you couldn't think of a better question and you are asking a question just for the sake of it. You can ask general questions related to the culture of the company or the benefits the company offers, but don't ask a question just because you have to.

Keep in mind that specific questions related to the job responsibilities always show you as more interested in the position rather than asking very general questions. Therefore, prepare the questions you will ask before going to your interview.

14) What are some common mistakes in interviews and how do I avoid them?

As I mentioned above, talking only about your career goals and what you are interested in is a mistake. You should always emphasize that you are going to bring different values to an organization, since that's what generally employers are interested in.

Some people do not ask questions during interviews. That's also considered a mistake by employers. You should always ask questions during interviews and prepare these questions in advance.

Also, not studying the company before the interview is a big mistake. You should learn as much information as you can related to that company before going to your interview. This can be anything related to the company, such as its projects, its clients, its departments, or its locations.

Moreover, you should always dress up for an interview because it's always better to dress up rather than dress down. Ideally, you should wear a suit for any interview even if you are interviewing with a technical company and even if the company has a casual dress code, since you are not its employee yet and you need to look your best. Therefore, you should never dress casually for any interview. You should always go dressed up. Remember, it is always better to be dressed up rather than down.

Furthermore, don't oversell yourself just because you want a job and try to be relevant to the company you are interviewing with. For example, once I tried to oversell myself to a web-based company during an interview. I mentioned that I worked on Wall Street and told them that was one of my proudest accomplishments. I thought it was a big accomplishment for a twenty-three-year-old to start her career with a client on Wall Street. Well, I forgot one thing! I was interviewing with a web company and not with a financial institution! The company was not interested whether I worked on Wall Street or not. That meant nothing for them. This experience taught me that my background always has to match the needs of the company I am interviewing with, and that I should not brag about myself or try to oversell myself in any interview.

15) Should I ask for the business cards of the people I interviewed with?

Yes. You should ask for the business cards of your interviewers so you can follow up with a thank-you letter or e-mail, or add them to your LinkedIn contacts.

7 WHAT HAPPENS AFTER THE INTERVIEW (GOT AN OFFER, HOW TO NEGOTIATE THE OFFER)

You aced the interview using the techniques you learned in the previous chapter and, finally, the moment you had been waiting for arrived. You got the offer!

In this chapter, I will talk about what you should do after your interviews, how to evaluate an offer and negotiate it if you need to, and, finally, what you need to do before your first day at work.

After the interview:
After your interview, you should always follow up with a thank-you letter and show your gratitude to the people who interviewed you.

A thank-you letter or e-mail shows your appreciation to the other people who took the time to talk with you or to interview with you. Also, it shows that you are still interested in the position and maybe even more interested in it now as a result of the interview and meeting with the employees of the company and learning more about the company culture.

As I mentioned above, I've seen people lose a job offer just because they didn't send a thank-you letter, and you don't want that to happen to you.

Usually, in a week or two, the company should contact you if it wants to invite you for another round of interviews or if it is going to offer you a position. But if you don't hear back from your interviewers after two weeks, you can always follow up and ask when you should expect to hear from them. Hopefully, you will hear good news and you will get the offer you have been waiting for.

How to evaluate and negotiate an offer:
First of all, you should not evaluate the offer based only on salary information. The salary is important for many people, but you should also look for other benefits, such as how many paid holidays you will get per year or if you can work remotely some days during the work week or if you are getting any perks, for example, a gym membership discount or other discounts from other businesses such as phone-bill discounts or electronic-equipment discounts or travel discounts. You should then evaluate the offer as a whole package.

If the salary in the offer is below your expectations, you can always call the company and ask whether the offer is negotiable. The company will tell you whether it's negotiable. If it is not negotiable, you can always compare the offer with your previous salary or with industry standards to explain to the company why you want to negotiate your salary and why you think you are worth more. For example, you can say, "My previous salary was X, and I have a graduate-level degree, so I was planning to start working with a salary 15-20 percent higher than my previous one, since I have a master's degree now." Or you can cite labor statistics. You can say, "I looked up the labor statistics and they show that people earn X dollars for this kind of position, so can you please match your offer with what is listed here to be fair value."

However, don't forget that companies have specified budgets for their hires, so even though you try to negotiate with them, it may not always work, but still it is worth trying. In one of the offers that I received when I was graduating with my MBA, the salary was well below my expectations, so I used the above approach to negotiate it. The company increased it by 4 percent, but it was still below my expectations, so I rejected that offer and kept on interviewing with other companies.

If the offer is not open to negotiation and you are not happy with it, then it's up to you to decide if you are going to take it or not. But as I stated, salary information shouldn't be the only criterion on which to base your decision, and you should always look at it as a whole package. Still, if you are not going to be happy working with a salary under your expectations, then maybe you should move on like I did and keep on interviewing.

You can also ask when they would review your performance for a raise, because companies sometimes do six-month reviews. If a six-month review is available and the company tells you at that stage that it is happy with your performance, you may get a promotion or an increase in your salary. However, some companies may not do a review for a pay increase for up to two years, so you should ask when you can get a raise if you accept this offer and what is the average percentage for raises within the company.

Another important element to look for in the offer is whether it has the condition of H-1B sponsorship. If it's not in the offer, you should ask the company if it is definitely going to sponsor you for an H-1B visa and why it is not stated in the offer. The company may forget to state this information or it may hire you for a trial period for a few months with your OPT authorization before deciding whether to sponsor you for an H-1B visa. Whatever the case, you should always ask about the H-1B sponsorship condition if it is not listed clearly in the offer. You should know whether they are going to sponsor you so you can decide on your strategy.

Deciding to accept or reject the offer:
Usually, all offers have a deadline. This deadline depends on the company. Companies generally give you a few days or a week to decide on the offer. On the other hand, some companies can give you a month to decide..

If you are also waiting to hear back from other companies or you are not sure whether to accept or reject an offer, you can ask for an extension of the deadline. You can say, "I also interviewed with company X and I am expecting their response. I really want to work for you, but I want to consider all of my options before I make my final decision. Can you please give me more time to think about this offer?" I'm sure most companies will extend the deadline and give you more time.

Most students wonder if they can accept an offer and still continue looking for other jobs. The answer is no. It's not ethical to accept a job offer and still look for other jobs. It doesn't look good on you.

If you accept an offer from a company, it means that you are going to start working for that company, and the company stops looking for other candidates. Let's say you accept an offer and still continue looking for other jobs and you find another job that you like better. If you go back to the first company and say, "I decided not to work for you because I accepted another offer," it doesn't look good on you. This shows that you are not being ethical. It also puts the company in a bad situation, since it has to look for another candidate for that position. Don't accept an offer and still continue looking for other jobs.

You should always inform the company whether you will accept or reject its offer. You can inform the company via e-mail, over the phone, or face-to-face. It really depends on what you are comfortable with.

Get ready for your employment start date:
In order to get ready for your first day of employment, you should stay in touch with the HR personnel. You should ask them if you need to fill out any documents or provide any personal information, such as your passport ID page or a photo or work-authorization documents.

They will probably e-mail you and ask you to bring some documentation with you on your first day of work or ask you to e-mail them before your first day. Some companies even give you a computer in advance before your first day.

You should always check back with the company because every company is different, but most companies require you to fill out some paperwork before you start, so it's always best to be prepared.

Also, if you have never worked in the United States before, you need to apply and get a social security number (SSN) in order to be able to start working. An SSN is a nine-digit number that identifies you. You should get an SSN for tax purposes before your start date so companies can pay you using your SSN and then you can also file your taxes with that SSN.

It's easy to get an SSN. You should go to the social security office, fill out some forms, show your job offer to prove that you are going to work, and then in a couple of weeks the agency will mail your SSN card to you.

First day of work:
You never know what to expect on your first day of work. It depends on the company, but usually you can expect a company orientation. You will probably meet with your managers, with your team mates, and with other people who are going to work with you. You'll probably get a computer and get oriented to the company.

On the first day of work, I recommend going dressed up in a suit because you never know what to expect. Even if the dress code is casual, you should still go there dressed up at least in business casual if you think wearing a suit will be too much. Remember it's always better to be dressed up than dressed down.

Some companies have an onboarding process to help new hires get adapted to the company more easily. This is a process in which a company makes you feel welcome to the company. It's similar to the orientation process that you went through when you first started college in the United States.

The onboarding process can include being issued with a company computer, meeting with people that you are going to work with, doing training related to the company's culture, learning where the cafeteria is, and learning about the company's facilities. However, not every company has an onboarding process. Smaller companies, especially, do not have this process. Usually, big and midsize companies have an onboarding process, but every company tries its best to make you feel welcome and to onboard you to your new position so you can be productive as early as you can.

APPENDIX

Six Things You Need to Unlearn:

1) I can use the same resume that I have been using in my country to apply for jobs in the United States. Wrong! Every country has a different resume/cv format.

2) I can work in any job I want in the United States. Wrong! You can only apply for and work in jobs related to your major.

3) I have two semesters until I graduate, why do I have to start looking for a job so early? Companies won't be interested in me. Wrong! You should start the job-search process as early as possible. Two semesters before graduation is the ideal time to start searching for a full-time job.

4) It is enough if I apply for jobs only on the Internet and do nothing else. Wrong! You should always network and try to get to know the employees of your target companies if you want to land an interview, or you can use LinkedIn and other social media tools to connect with employers.

5) Companies recruit students only after they graduate. Wrong! This may be true in some other countries, but it is certainly not true in the United States. Big enterprises in the United States recruit students as early as their junior year in school.

6) Any of my skills and achievements is applicable to all companies. Wrong! For example, if you are looking for a job as a financial analyst in a finance company, then you should emphasize your previous finance classes and internships in the finance field, since this background is relevant to the job that you are applying for. You should not be emphasizing how good you are at programming in Java—though you can certainly talk about it, this should not be your emphasis.

Key Takeaways from this Book:

1) Start the job-search process as early as possible:

Michael Miller, President of Culture Adapt, says that "if you're a senior or a graduate student trying to get into the work world, you really have to start immediately when you arrive. You have to start building your skills, understanding the differences in culture and actually start networking."

When I first came to the US, I didn't know companies were hiring in the fall semester for a full-time position because in my country (I am from Turkey) when we are looking for jobs as college students, we usually look in the spring semester.

In Turkey, if you are going to graduate in May, you usually start looking for a full-time job in February, March, or sometimes April because companies don't hire you before you graduate. They only hire you if you are close to graduation.

However, in the US it's the opposite. They can even hire you a year in advance. If you make an internship with them, they can hire you right after your internship, even if you didn't complete your degree and you still have one year left for your graduation. That's why I need you to start the job-search process as early as possible."

2) Never underestimate the importance of networking (including face-to-face networking and social media networking.):

You should never underestimate the importance of networking, including face-to-face networking and social media networking. In my case, I got most of my job offers through going to job fairs and information sessions. I also got a job offer from a company that I applied to through LinkedIn. Thus, you should always use social media and face-to-face networking.

3) Know your work-authorization rights in the United States and let the employers know about these if you need to:

You should know your work-authorization rights in the United States, a subject I discussed fully in my opening chapter. Lucy Amello, Associate Director of Graduate Career Services at Bentley University, says that "students have to definitely educate themselves on their work-authorization rights because that will help them with educating the employers as well because some employers are not educated in that either."

You should educate employers if they do not know that international students can work in the United States, because some employers don't know whether they can hire international students. Fifty-five percent of the international students who took my survey believe that employers know that they can hire international students. However, the reality is most of them don't know whether they can. When I attended job fairs, employers would asked me, "You are an international student. Can you work in the US?" In response, I would educate them by saying, "Yes, we can work in the US because everybody gets work authorization in the US for a year, at least, once they complete their degrees, and this work authorization can be extended with a work visa called H-1B."

4) Know when the companies you are targeting recruit:

I also want you to know when your target companies are recruiting, because some companies, especially big enterprises, recruit in the fall semester. For example, the Big Four accounting firms or consulting firms or financial institutions usually recruit in the fall semester. Small and midsize companies usually recruit in the spring semester.

5) Make sure your resume is only one page long unless you are a PhD student or someone with at least eight to nine years' work experience:

Make sure your resume is only one page long unless you are a PhD student or someone with at least eight to nine years of experience, because, as I illustrated with an example in a previous chapter, it may look bad if your resume is longer than one page.

6) Be relevant to the company you are interviewing with.

Always be relevant to the company you are interviewing with. For example, I was interviewed by a web company and asked what my accomplishments were. I told my interviewers that I worked for high-profile clients on Wall Street. Then, I noticed that they were not interested in my accomplishments on Wall Street, because that is a finance-related field and I was interviewing with a web company.

We tend to think that any of our accomplishments is valuable. It is valuable for you, but it may not always be valuable for others.

7)   Learn how to turn your disadvantages into advantages.

You should learn how to turn your disadvantages into advantages. For example, as I mentioned, companies value diversity in the United States. If you are bilingual or know three or four languages, you should emphasize this during interviews.

Most international students know three or four languages. That's a very big advantage, and you should use this advantage in addition to your international background to emphasize your diversity and the diverse knowledge or perspective that you have.

8)   Learn what employers would like to hear from you in interviews and answer accordingly.

Employers do not always want to learn about you, but they want to learn about what you are going to bring to the table. Michael Miller of Culture Adapt agrees that students should focus on the value that they can bring to a company. I also think that you should always emphasize what values you are going to bring to the organization and not just talk about your career goals and interests.

Key Takeaways from Professional Counselors:

1)   Understand the US job market and understand what areas are hiring international students in America. (Lucy Amello, associate director of graduate career services at Bentley University)

2) Get involved in your college. Join student clubs, take leadership opportunities, and build your resume early on. (Oktay Sekercisoy, director for international partnership development at Binghamton University)

3) If the international student enters into a company and does not adapt to the corporate culture and blend and be flexible to fit in, it's uncomfortable within the company. It's not a global mix. Of course you hold onto your own culture, but it's the old saying: When in Rome, do as the Romans. It is incumbent on the international student to realize that they must become a global citizen and fit in. (Wendy D'Ambrose, director of graduate career services at Bentley University)

4) The best way to find a job in the US is by connecting with decision makers and getting specific in what you want to do. Once you build a relationship with them, you can start the immigration talk, the job talk, and people aren't going to reject you immediately just because you need an H-1B sponsorship. (Michael Miller, president of Culture Adapt)

5) The participation of the student is very, very important. The big majority of students, as you know, if they are from other countries, are still struggling with the language and that is very, very important to speak it, to practice it, to make it better every single day that they are here so that they will come across as educated and very fluent in English. (Lucy Amello, associate director of graduate career services at Bentley University)

6) Understand that you are bringing a different perspective to this country or the organization that

you are in or the school that you are in. You should trust that you are a great asset and great value to any organization you go because you are bringing two different countries' perspectives and cultures to that organization. That's invaluable. You cannot learn that in school. (Oktay Sekercisoy, director for international partnership development at Binghamton University)

7) Don't tell corporations that you are desperate and you will do anything for free. International students must understand corporate employers cannot bring an international student on for free because it is against federal fair labor standards. That would smack of exploitation. Nonprofits can bring an international student on as a volunteer. Start-ups can bring an international student on as a volunteer, but it's very important that international students understand corporations, established businesses, can't bring you on as a volunteer. (Wendy D'Ambrose, director of graduate career services at Bentley University)

8) With international students, I think one of the biggest issues is networking and getting over that fear of talking to complete strangers. Maybe it's your accent. Maybe you don't know English that well, but just getting over that initial fear will change the rest of your life. (Michael Miller, president of Culture Adapt)

CONCLUSION

I have shared my knowledge and experience that helped me in landing a sponsored job in the United States. I hope you find this information helpful and useful. You may hear similar advice and stories from other people, but in the end it is up to you how to use this information and to put it into action.

Please also don't forget that finding a job is a combination of many different factors, including the economy and the job market. Sometimes, even though you do everything right, you may not get the results you want due to these external factors. I always believe that if a door closes, another door opens. Although you believe that you did everything right and still could not find a sponsored job in the United States, don't think of this as the end of the world. This only means that a bigger and better opportunity is waiting for you somewhere else in the world, and maybe you will be much happier with that opportunity and you will come to regret that you put yourself under so much stress during your senior year in the United States. I wish you all the best with your job search and hope you all achieve the success you deserve in your careers...

LIKE OUR FACEBOOK PAGE TO STAY
CONNECTED AND GET FREE TIPS FOR FINDING
A JOB IN THE UNITED STATES

You can like our Facebook page by going to:

https://www.facebook.com/makeyouramericandreamareality

Or by scanning the below QR code with your phone: